THE HOUSE
—OF—
MEN

poems
stewart shaw

GLASS LYRE PRESS

Copyright © 2019 Stewart Shaw
Paperback ISBN: 978-1-941783-59-7

All rights reserved: except for the purpose of quoting brief passages for review, no part of this book may be reproduced or transmitted in any form or by any means, electronic or mechanical, including photocopying, recording, or by any information storage and retrieval system, without permission in writing from the publisher.

Design & Layout: Steven Asmussen
Cover Art: Nia Perry
Copyediting: Elizabeth Nichols

Glass Lyre Press, LLC
P.O. Box 2693
Glenview, IL 60025
www.GlassLyrePress.com

THE
HOUSE
OF
MEN

Contents

Rusty Like Blood	1
Holes	2
The Geophagist	4
THE DOGS OF CALVARY	5
CONFESSIONS #14	7
APOSTASY #1	8
Apostasy #2	9
The Salesman	11
Crossing Over	12
In a canyon, the man sings to the beautiful ladies—	13
Holy, holy	14
All I know about love and sex, I learned from my parents	15
I have been poorly indoctrinated	19
The House of Men	20
He wants to read me	21
Nana Loves Venus Hottentot, Kwaku Loves Kunta	22
Olly olly oxen free	25
daddy sings us goodbyes	26
SECRETS	28
CONFESSION #69	29
How to Make a Faggot	30
Four Ways of Looking at a Black Boy	31
at the edge of the world we look over and pray for wings	32
If a blk woman, magical only in white fantasies, screams in the night, does anyone hear her, does she hear herself? Do we care?	33
CONFESSION #1	34
Acknowledgments	37
About the Author	39

RUSTY LIKE BLOOD

He

don't sing to me

no more. Don't

bring baubles of soul and prayer

in his mouth. His

cast iron throat has stopped

cooking. I am left

hungry.

When black men leave, they leave.

missing parts, arms

legs, spaces between ribs

never growing or dying. I

am in the black leaving

of his departure; it

sits on my tongue,

the taste

bitter, rusty

Like blood.

HOLES

i.

Men are always falling
Into holes
Into ether-less spaces
While walking
Buying cigarettes
Pretending they are circus performers
walking tightropes without a net.

ii.

Father fell into a hole in the side of a mountain
sooty miners
scrabbling around in the dark
searching for coal that held
their livelihoods
their deaths.

iii.

A brother crawled out her mother's womb
his limbs the twisted fervor of a Kansas tornado,
lungs clogged with prairie dust
leaving no room for air -
soon he fell into the grave exchanging
one hole for another.

iv.

She ran from the land of holes.

Escaping buffalo, the Kickapoo
scrubbing and cleaning
for the nice Jewish doctor,
a life as flat and monotonous
as the open plains.

She ran
from and to lovers
a husband, her first and only.
He fell
into a hole of his own.
despair, failure cracked him open
exposing his jaundiced liver, a heart
that beat out conflicting rhythms of melancholia
and a late-night two-step.

v.

He dropped deeper into the bottle, into
self-loathing succumbing to his own dark
plummet.

After him she gave up tying herself
to the dreams of a man.

With dirt under her nails, she dug
her way out again. *Ah,*
she thought, *light.*

vi.

Mother,
whose arms were big as a man's had
taught her how to use a shovel,
how to fill in gaps in the earth,
how to throw over her left shoulder
all bad juju that collected around her ankles,
how to crawl up,
out, how to dance
around holes and ditches and
still want to live.

THE GEOPHAGIST

She says her heart is a stone / when pregnant / looking for salts / she swallowed an ocean / a pebble found / its way in / birth was a tender tearing / a world sliding / between her legs / later the emptiness / calcifying / in her chest

The recipe said/
dig deep/
into muddy banks/red cliffs/California soil/rocky and parched/
eat/taste through salt/sweet/burnt hands/burnt bodies/sweat/
there are hollers left/in the hills/to be digested/then spat out/
tender mercies/curses
left/in rocks/ribboned with tongue marks/
festooned with/faded directions/
to the keeping place

Chalk / holds answers / lime / iron / magnesium / spices informing / and when there are no more words / in the walls / within the outlines / beneath feckless paint chips / behind plaster / swallow pebbles / fill the belly / with graveled talk and whispers

She hopes there is truth / in the telling / red clay / dug up under full moon / tucked gently under lip / fingered-rounded balls / swallowed whole / helps the blood flow strong / limbs aching for travel move

She swallows Bibles / scripture melt / beneath her tongue / paper cuts crisscross / throat / ink / lines lips / black and blacker / lacquered finished / the covers / tree-lined with names / she leaves for last / till there is no room in her chest

And when she could find no more words / one by one she ate / her fingers / first nail then flesh / bone / maybe there was something left inside / a dream / a question / would flow free / with the blood

THE DOGS OF CALVARY
—dem bones dem bones dem bones

Our secrets overtakes us
we ride up the hill
hounds on our tails
and I look back to see his smile
in a dog's grin.

Today I will find the bone in me
that was my father
pluck it out and throw it
to the dogs.
Pick my teeth with his ear bones
Spit. Beneath my teeth - stapes, incus, malleus
crushed to deafness
still play back memories, coat my throat.

My mother
who didn't take me to the funeral
looks away distracted
will not bring father now to the altar
will bury the memory of him
deep in the bone pile.   His
ossuary never to be opened.

My brother
named after him
the same tilting smile
same tripping tongue
knows the taste of sedition
gnaws his arm off to free himself
from the responsibility of a name
throws it on the pile
in the family graveyard
with the others.
But he is blessed or cursed
It grows back.

Our secrets overtakes us
we ride up the hill hounds on our tails
and I look back to see his smile
in a dog's grin.

In the house of bones
I whistle to keep away ghosts, blow
out dust. In my mouth
saliva taste like an Otis Redding
song, I sing
in my father's voice.

CONFESSIONS #14

What does daddy smell like?

I have waited
in too many locker rooms
back alleys
for his Saturday hair cut odor-
bay rum, sweat, Lucky Strikes
cheap liquor.

I have licked skin
to find his scent.

APOSTASY #1

My father who aren't
In heaven or hell,
Or at home cooking on Sundays,
Cast-iron skillet filled
With onions, bacon, fried potatoes,   blasphemer's
Tears -
Drops of communion bourbon,
Or Whiteport - an extra look at
glory;

. . .Where
Art thou? Where
Have you hidden yourself this
Time?

APOSTASY #2

Daddy
Was a ditch-digger. When
he was below
He said he could feel
The creep of time across his shoulders, down
His 6foot2 frame, through
his tremulous body,
Through swilling gut
To his traveling feet
 Stuck in one place.

Down below see level
Memory wavers. There
Is no chain of consequence – all
That went before, holds
Little thrall or meaning. It is easy
To forget. How you came to this
Place, this circumstance; dig
And dug is all there is.   One by one
He teaches us kids
How to dig a hole.

First he says
Determine why you are digging –
Garden, fence post, a secret tunnel form
Dream to reality
Where underground utilities lines
Are – map out the ley lines
Between ground zero/home/grocery and liquor stores/
Nirvana and back. Then find
The right tool:
for soil a shovel or spade
cement, use jackhammer, backhoe. Always
wear gloves
save the hands
from blisters, calluses; keep them
soft for caressing, holding hands. Now
dig.

Empty the space of dirt, fill it with your
Body, the brown of skin taking
its place. Dig.

THE SALESMAN

Says boys are born of Immaculate Conception
the women smile,
Spread for him and then they tumble out
full grown with teeth and a hunger.

Says he's going out to buy some cigarettes.   Men are smoke.
Laughs into the wind. Mouths,
my love is toxic, no one person can hold it
and stay unscarred.

In the house of long counts
Boys count days behind glass
Number dents in empty beds still holding
A man's smell, his imprint, stains off-gassing his name.

The Salesman says   I am dead,
A boy answers   even death is
Abandonment and knows that he is being
Teased again with a leaving.

At one point the mothers bought his lies, ingested his idea of romance, tasted it from his lips, sipped the tenderness and strength of his comings and goings; fed his lines to their boys. Now they feign forgetfulness of his name, his face, his touch. The boys try not to forget that they were fathered.

CROSSING OVER

1.
Black is deep waters.
Bone deep.
White pearls of bleeding.
Feeding fish

2.
Shark infested waters
Tumble. Echoes.
lay in my throat
bask on my tongue come

3.
Nights by the angry ocean
Leaves restless bones
at my door. I
Sleepwalk.

4.
After the crossing
my people never
took to water. Every river
pond or pool holds teeth.

6.
I wonder can chalk
withstand salt water. Can
bodies gone for centuries
uphold their outlines?

7.
God won't trouble the water
we stir it clean
make our bed
of its white-capped linens.

IN A CANYON, THE MAN SINGS TO THE BEAUTIFUL LADIES—

along the banks, watch
for the man who howls.
He will bring down the stars
across your back- welts that burn, yet sparkle.

He wants you to call him
Father, for you to howl with him, wants
forgiveness
for chasing down dreams held within crescent moons,
for lacing stars inside the houses of
cooing doves who tremble
excitedly in his traps, for
sprinkling stars down the backs
of other fatherless watchers.

He wants
forgiveness for being
creator and destroyer.
For being able to howl.

Do not forgive, tears
cannot bring absolution.
Wait, hear the water rush,
listen to the sounds
in the night air,
know only one thing
You cannot howl, will not howl.

HOLY, HOLY

It is said,
cleanliness is next
to Godliness. I
do not know my god
or his name
there are
one hundred or
a thousand ways to call,
to reach Him.
I rinse, cleanse, purge
throw out all the old news
old places that he has touched
in his last disguise.

Holy, holy
water scented and blessed drips
from me like salvation and
with this I lubricate my soul
prepare the way
for him to come, come into
me, come unto me. Come
this way, come.

ALL I KNOW ABOUT LOVE AND SEX, I LEARNED FROM MY PARENTS

down

on my knees

in front of him

in the bright lights

of our room

studying his hardness

his erect

upstanding nature

I think of daddy

bring him here

with me

hear him say

the road through, son

is through hard work.

He

teaches me, I learn of

achy flesh

muscles turgid from digging ditches

for hours and years on end.

Staying power.

I bring my mama here
to my knees
smiling as we work
it out of our systems. I
hear a choir. She
could sing the good time
blues with the best. My
voice rises

I once heard
my daddy and mama
sexing hard
like after work
on Fridays when
there is nothing left
but release.

All I have learned
about love
I have learned
from them.

If Cliff and Claire

Huxtable fucked,

knowing that sometimes

making love was the devout

praying into empty hands,

if they left the cult

of respectability

behind,

they would have done it like

my parents

with shouts and hollers, rolling

all night long.

Always

a smile

after.

I have seen

this dick many times,

a hundred

a thousand

always the same taste

never varying

just like my Father Knows Best

daddy

who came home

to my Donna Reed mama

the same time each workday

wearing the same uniform

smelling of the same heady

ditch digger's sweat.

I am down here

on my knees

mouth full of

sacred moments. I

look for what falls out-

a prayer, an echo

of Friday nights

a benediction

a thanks.

I HAVE BEEN POORLY INDOCTRINATED

I still wear sin like a second skin I am Eve in all of her questioning,
Lillith refusing to bow down
return to her mantel. I want to take Jesus as a lover, but
cannot infiltrate his coterie of male hangers-on, I am bad with piety and blind belief, cant
always see much beyond my body. Yet I still want Jesus, he seems the perfect lover - thoughtful,
passionate and able
to rise again and again.

I am hell-bound for my lack of devotion, too wedded to the ground and not the sky.
If I can feel it, I know it is real. The sky is for seagulls and robins not fragile egos looking for
companionship and humble
connections.

I have never felt my father, so he is not real, pictures can be faked, a name given to smoke. Mama, she is real and holds my faith; I have seen her wooden cross, pulled the splinters from her back as I tried to hold it up for her on tender mornings when she begged for more than salvation.

I dream of Jesus though,
want to take him away from Judas -   the only man he trusted enough to give his life to. I know their private moments were always filled with acts of giving and taking. I want to give my life.

I make a lousy saint, but I think of Jesus too much
so I am also a lousy sinner.

THE HOUSE OF MEN

There is no touching   in the house of men just wrestler moves power take downs no
touching no removing of veils to tenderness
I am embattled trained in the ways of slipping touch trained by a skilled general in the war against
gentle stroke and caress and of binding the wound before the cut
the tongue and the eye and the heart can lie   deceive the senses into believing

they are real   how many times has he said I love you just to
disappear how many how many heartfelt gestures turned to dust after midnight ardor
this house of men is bankrupt has no doors or windows we all sleep
on barren floors face to back to back to   enslaved to dreams of doing as signs of love
doing
as gift more powerful than the touch that seeps through bone to spirit to DNA healing
lineage   the house of men sits in light   full of praying   hands coated with grief praying
to become doctors fakirs psychic healers

the house of men is filled   with boys

with babble the talking outside of the lines of hollow speech the   house
has age but no wisdom age but no men inside
always morning never afternoon or night   just men begetting boy begetting boy begetting men

HE WANTS TO READ ME

Daddy is calling from the other side
Or wherever daddies call from
When their echoes cease.
        I am paper
Thin and unread, He calls
to set my edges
Ablaze, to see how fast
I burn.

He wants to read
Me, calls me cocksucker. I smile
An orphaned smile
Think there is something
Subversive and powerful in knowing oneself. He
Never smiles in my visions.

My older brother got his name.
Space and questions and a need for closeness
My birthright.
I still navigate ancestral
Waters, still
let him call me
Names, let
Him
Call.

NANA LOVES VENUS HOTTENTOT, KWAKU LOVES KUNTA

During the Middle Passage
through horror and cries for home, through
stench, and death,
in cramped dark spaces, chains and stains
on souls more corrosive than hate, passions
were kindled, desires lived; hands
were roamed across aching backs
to ease kink and sorrow.

Women
in rows -
once fertile fields now gone barren-
fingered out lice and
dried vomit, unbraided knots of hurt
from napped heads twisted with death,
fondled breasts suckling life back
into their hollows.
Became lost in their own
journeys.

Men aligned belly to back
chanted
to sleeping gods, whispered
hunting stories
crooned love songs deep
into the splintered ears
of their neighbors. Did not
worry about tribe or clan
just succor. Cried
droughts away,
washed red burning backs with
gentle kisses.

In dark,
fetid and thick with
lamentations, deep
in the bowels of boats, someone
blew kisses,
tongued moans
blew kisses
tongued resurrection
blew kisses
like revolution
tongued healing
licking whip lines.
Blew kisses
pushing ancestors into
foul spaces filled with bereavement.
Tongued home
In semi-circles
down spines,
blew kisses
into ears crumbling
under the weight
of death's rattle.   Tongued
the darkness bright.

Kwaku, spelling
in darkness
Kunta's name
along the raised mountain
of a back,
blew kisses
tongued midnight air
sung lullabyes.

Knew water flowed two ways

Nana, arm across
Saartjie's belly,

blew her a kiss
hung gentle memories
in a womb still full of prayers
let go of sick, felt
no roll or tumble of sea
just knew firmament.
just felt rounded
hallowed ground.

Olly olly oxen free

i want to walk the California coast

with my Father, take his
hand as we traverse oceanside cliffs, stick
wild yellow yarrow behind his ear, stick native grasses in my hair, make of him an elemental,

carve

his name along the ridge of the cliff's spine, shout his name into the misting air and have the sea breezes throw it back at us. Remember who you are i will say as i ride his back through gully, pine choked arroyo and ravine.

The first prayer ever uttered was a whisper to the Mother, even when she is pushed aside for the second prayer to the father, she hangs on feeding the tendrils of memory.

Father in his wistful way must be reminded of place,   anchored.

So i scream out tithes to him.
Mother always know her way back, she has left a trail of

laughter,

tears and

blood to mark her way.

Father has never learned   to monitor his steps.

daddy sings us goodbyes

1-
He mixed rhythm
& blues with his gin.
Stirred it until
It was a party

Caught cat-fish on Fridays
swam through ditches
on his way home.

Daddy
through breath, hot
from Lucky Strikes,
told his mama when
he left home the first time - you
still ma girl. Told mama-when
he got home, the second time
baby, you, still ma girl.

2-
He is memory
sepia toned,
hands reaching down, out
of nowhere to
collect me- he
is ghost haunting
walls and dreams -
an occasional family
picnic.

3-
Daddy thought he was Otis Redding
as he sung with the radio
that was perched on top of the refrigerator.
Wanted to taste the red clay
layered in the music,
wanted to be reminded of home,

the honey cloistered in the soil there.
His dreams
made him forget us for moments
and hours, got him lost in his souring cup,
turned his insides black and rebellious.

4-
And mama, us
kids waited.
Maybe for the real Otis
to slip in behind daddy's singing,
come and lay
hands on
tiny heads napped
like Bible verses,
ease us into light; keep daddy happy
when he wasn't singing, or
maybe when he was.

SECRETS

I don't think he wanted me to know him / so he left / right after I was born / right before I could say / I love you or daddy / before the crust around the Earth in my chest could harden and lock him in / he was gone / taking with him my older brother / returning him back from where the dead live / back to the family / only once he had used up his youth / my brother came back gray and tired / speaking in the riddled tongue of the aged / he had to relearn the concept of touch / how the sprig of a finger can blossom on skin / open up closed spaces just beneath / make unyielding hearts bend / my father had touched my brother in hidden places and left within him secrets / maybe this is the way of oldest sons / they bear scars / the weight of history / my brother keeps his secrets / my mother does not make him tell / nor will she open up her silences to me / it is me / who folks say look like the man / yet I am anchor-less with no secrets of my own to tell.

CONFESSION #69

He glazes my back
with his
A) permeable
B) impermeable
C) lazy
Tongue
All depends on the day and
Hour, tilt of moon
Rising sun.

I am not for want of company
Still I look under
Cushions for change
Left behind, pray
He comes back

He is Mufasa, no
Mandingo, NAH
Daddy?

HOW TO MAKE A FAGGOT

Breast milk
From a praying mother

Lipstick kisses
Avon Purple Plum

Smoke from a
Virginia Slim

Caul fat
Lightly placed over the face

Laughter
Cause we all need that

Tear cried over
A good man. Cause we all need that

A stereotype
A stereotype

A love is love
Wherever you find it attitude

A rolling stone stuck
Between a rock and a soft place

Do not stir
Or shake just shimmy

A punch to the gut
A punch to the face

An attentive father
Who stays home

A Superman costume
For Halloween

A Mae West costume
For his 6th birthday

A punch to the face
A punch to the gut

An absent father
Who stays home

a grandmother who knows
her baby is touched
by god by his son and don't care
who else touches him
as long as it is tender.

FOUR WAYS OF LOOKING AT A BLACK BOY

1 -
His nose drooped
eyes sagged and
his face tried to run
away from both

2 -
Fire, fire burning; douse
the flame
extinguish the heat. He
was warned, life
was a cold place

3 -
Garbage bags stood
In his eyes, a
Broom
In his hands

4 -
In the cold
of morning, his
face would become frost
bitten and cracked, if
he chipped away
he would still be

at the edge of the world we look over and pray for wings
(for the 9 who died in the Charleston Church Shootings 6/17/2015)

beneath this nave of trees
pine and juniper

beneath sky
cloud and star

hunting is not allowed
no logger with axe
and saw to be found

Let prayer happen
nine voices strong
      singing in the range of wind
           and bird

Let dust
heavy knee prints endure
till rain and river in their rightful time
        wash all blood   away

If a blk woman, magical only in white fantasies, screams in the night, does anyone hear her, does she hear herself? Do we care?

She is an ambulance   siren
And well
She is big   lugging
'round the wounded like a nervous
Tick   she can't say no
Again, and again and

She is siren, a wail
Of ambulance   lugging
'round the wounded
Again
and again, and she
Can't say
No
A nervous   tick

On her wail
She brings them home   wounded
And ticking
To heal.
Again and again
They never say no

CONFESSION #1

Georgie/was never taught
Not to kiss/the boys/how
To keep his secrets/on the low/speak
No evil or truths/keep his heart
On lockdown/that
No man should bare/his vulnerabilities/leave
The heart open to scrutiny

His heart beats/
With the tinkling of a coin/explodes/
Graffiti over walls/tattooing
Bellies/backs/smiles of lonely/
Strangers/so many
Pretty colors/make
The men cry.

ACKNOWLEDGMENTS

Thanks to the editors of the following journals in which some of these poems have appeared, sometimes in slightly different versions:

Serendipity Literary Magazine: "House of Men," "Nana Loves Venus Hottentot, Kunta Loves Kwaku"

African American Review: "Daddy Sings Us Goodbyes"

I want to thank all of those who have believed in me even when I didn't believe in myself and wasn't writing a thing. Sonya Smith who always said "even thinking about writing is writing." L. Lamar Wilson for always believing I was a poet, although I showed little proof. Marion Smith for being a great reader, BWC for just being himself. Michael Stewart for being my rock. Charles Shaw for being there unconditionally. My family for always quietly rooting me on and supporting me even when I rarely let them into my writing world; thanks Karen, Thoette, Howard, Yvette, Viola, Stephanie and Felecia. Cagney, Kateema Lee, Kevin Mwachiro all for being that friend. Thanks to all the poets I have ever confabbed with and workshopped with. Thanks to the daughter I never thought I would have, but always wanted. Thanks to my daughter Sakile, for allowing me to walk along side of you on your journey. LOVE

Thanks to the one person who fully, totally and without reservation believed in me and always showed up when needed- my Mama.

ABOUT THE AUTHOR

S. Shaw was born and raised by a single, widowed mother in Berkeley, California. He is the seventh of eight kids and was always the introspective mama's boy; shy and unsure of his footing. With this background, of course he would become a poet. He has always written stories and poems, but never believed he could be an author.

He has been a public librarian in different urban libraries, an ice cream maker. He is a father of one daughter, a son, brother and friend, believes in magic and Bigfoot.

Stewart studied creative writing as an undergraduate at San Francisco State University focusing in fiction, and has attended writing conferences in various African nations, as well as attending writer retreats trying to find where his talents lie. His poems have been published in *African American Review, Temenos Literary Journal, The Missing Slate,* as well as a short story in *Mighty Real: An Anthology of African American Same Gender Loving Writing.* It wasn't until he applied for and got accepted into the *Cave Canem* writers retreat for poets of African descent and became a fellow, did Stewart believe he could write poetry for others to read and not to be hidden away in a journal.

exceptional works to replenish the spirit

Glass Lyre Press is an independent literary publisher interested in technically accomplished, stylistically distinct, and original work. Glass Lyre seeks diverse writers that possess a dynamic aesthetic and an ability to emotionally and intellectually engage a wide audience of readers.

Glass Lyre's vision is to connect the world through language and art. We hope to expand the scope of poetry and short fiction for the general reader through exceptionally well-written books, which evoke emotion, provide insight, and resonate with the human spirit.

Poetry Collections
Poetry Chapbooks
Select Short & Flash Fiction
Anthologies

www.GlassLyrePress.com

www.ingramcontent.com/pod-product-compliance
Lightning Source LLC
Chambersburg PA
CBHW030135100526
44591CB00009B/673